Phil H. LISTEMANN

Colour artwork : Clavework-graphics

Layout & project design : Phil Listemann

Copyright © Phil Listemann 2013, revised 2015

ISBN 978-2-918590-63-7

ACKNOWLEDGEMENTS

Alex Crawford, Chris Goss, Phil Jarrett, Andrew Thomas.

Edited by Phil H. Listemann

philedition@wanadoo.fr

www.RAF-IN-COMBAT.com

GLOSSARY OF TERMS

(CAN)/RAF : Canadian serving with the RAF
F/L : Flight Lieutenant
F/O : Flying Officer
F/Sgt : Flight Sergeant
Lt : Lieutenant
(NZ)/RAF : New Zealander serving with the RAF
P/O : Pilot Officer
RAF : Royal Air Force
RAP : Reserve Aircraft Park
RCAF : Royal Canadian Air Force

(SA)/RAF : South African serving with the RAF
Sgt : Sergeant
S/L : Squadron Leader
SOC : Struck of charge
Sqn : Squadron
W/C : Wing Commander
W/O : Warrant Officer

INTRODUCTION

Side view of one of 23 Fury Mk.IIs built by Hawker. K7275 is seen before its delivery to the RAF.

With the knowledge gained from the Intermediate and High Speed Fury Hawkers submitted an improved Fury design to the Air Ministry. One Fury, K1935, had been sent to the Kingston works and was fitted with a Kestrel IV engine and wheel spats. During trials at Martlesham Heath this aircraft reached a speed of 228mph. With an additional fuel tank in the fuselage this dropped to 223mph. The Air Ministry drafted Specification F.36 to cover this new design. An initial order of 23 Fury IIs (K7263-K7285 against contract 421941/35) was placed with the Kingston works and delivered between October and December 1936. A further order for 89 aircraft were subcontracted to General Aircraft at Hanworth and deliveries took place between July 1936 and April 1937 (K8218-K8306 against contract 419059/35) making a total production of 112 Mk.II for the RAF. With the entry of the Fury II the original Furies were now re-designated Fury I. In taking the production of the Mk.I in count, the RAF took charge in total 230 Furies over a six years period, between April 1931 and April 1937.

TECHNICAL DATA
FURY MK.II

Manufacturer and production:
23 by H.G. Hawker Engineering Co.
89 by General Aircraft Ltd.

Type :
Single-seat interceptor fighter.

Powerplant :
One 640 hp Rolls-Royce Kestrel VI twelve-cylinder inline liquid-cooled engine.
(525 hp Rolls-Royce Kestrel IIS for the Mk.I)

Fuel & Oil
Fuel (Imp Gal):
Normal capacity : 50 [227 l]

Oil (Imp Gal):
4.5 [20.5 l]

Dimensions :
Span : 30 ft 0-in [9,14 m]
Length : 26 ft 8-in [8,17 m]
Height : 10 ft 2-in [3,10 m]
Wing area : 251.8 sq ft [23,4 m²]

Weights :
Empty : 2,734 lb/1 242 kg - *Mk.I: 2,623 lb /1 190 kg*
Loaded : 3,609 lb/1 640 kg - *Mk.I 3,490 lb /1 583 kg*

Performance :
Max speed :
223 mph at 16,500 ft - *Mk.I 207 mph at 14,000 ft*
358 km/h at 5 000 m - *Mk.I 333 km/h at 4 250 m*

Service ceiling : 29,500 ft/8 950 m - *Mk.I 28,000 ft/8 500 m*
Normal range : 270 miles/435 km - *Mk.I 305 miles/490 km]*

Armament :
2 x 0.303-in [7.7 mm] Vickers II in the nose with 600 rpg.

DELIVERIES AND STRENGHT
FURY MK.II

Month (at last day)	Delivered	Total delivered	Op. Losses	Accident [1]	SOC	Available
July 36	6	6	-	-	-	6
August 36	-	6	-	-	-	6
September 36	9	15	-	-	-	15
October 36	24	39	-	-	-	39
November 36	15	54	-	-	-	54
December 36	15	69	-	-	-	69
January 37	24	93	-	2	-	91
February 37	18	111	-	1	-	108
March 37	-	111	-	-	-	108
April 37	1	112	-	2	-	107
May 37	-	112	-	3	-	104
June 37	-	112	-	1	-	103
July 37	-	112	-	-	-	103
August 37	-	112	-	1	-	102
.../...						
November 37	-	112	-	2	-	100
December 37	-	112	-	1	-	99
January 38	-	112	-	1	-	98
February 38	-	112	-	-	-	98
March 38	-	112	-	1	-	97
April 38	-	112	-	1	-	96
May 38	-	112	-	1	1	94
June 38	-	112	-	1	-	93
.../...						
September 38	-	112	-	1	-	92
October 38	-	112	-	3	-	89
November 38	-	112	-	2	-	87
December 38	-	112	-	1	-	86
.../...						
March 39	-	112	-	2	-	84
.../...						
June 39	-	112	-	2	19	63
July 39	-	112	-	-	1	62
.../...						
September 39	-	112	-	1	2	59
October 39	-	112	-	-	-	59
November 39	-	112	-	1	1	57
December 39	-	112	-	-	-	57
January 40	-	112	-	-	34	23
February 40	-	112	-	2	2	19
March 40	-	112	-	1	1	17
April 40	-	112	-	-	7	10
May 40	-	112	-	-	3	7
June 40	-	112	-	-	4	3
July 40	-	112	-	-	2	1
August 40	-	112	-	-	-	-
September 40	-	112	-	-	1	-

[1] In case of accident, the month of the accident was selected above the struck of charge date (SOC).

THE UNITS

The last Furies built were not assigned at first but stored instead like K8303, K8300 and K8301. They are here seen in a hangar at No.3 ASU (Aircraft Storage Unit) in 1937.

No.25 Squadron
October 1936 - October 1937

After having the second user of the Fury Mk.I, No.25 Squadron was selected to become the first one for the Fury Mk.II. These were delivered on the 2nd of October 1936 and consisted of K7263-K7276 belonging to the batch built by Hawker. In November five more Fury IIs, K7277-K7281 were delivered. Another two, K7282 and K7283 were also received at a later date. During the year of use, two of these new Furies suffered engine failure. The first was K7267 on the 26th April 1937 obliging its pilot, Sgt Ernest W.J. Monk to make an emergency landing at Hawkinge but the aircraft overturned, fortunately without major injuries for the pilot. Later commissioned, Monk was eventually was killed on take-off on 21 November 1940, still serving the Squadron. The other occurred on the 3rd August (K7279); this time the pilot, P/O Lloyd K. Keith choose to make an emergency landing near Dymchurch, Kent, but here too, it ended badly for the Fury which hit a ditch in the process. The pilot was however badly injured and was sent to hospital and by the outbreak of wa, heb had selected to fly with the FAA. By October 1937 the Squadron was starting to be re-equipped with Hawker Demons and most of its Furies were passed on to No.41 Squadron.

No.73 Squadron
March 1937 - July 1937

When formed on 15 March 1937 at Mildenhall by using a nucleus of pilots from Nos.19 and 56 Squadrons' 'B' Flights, it

wasn't planned at first to equip No.73 Squadron with Furies but with Gladiators. But as the production of these was running slow fifteen Fury IIs were issued instead. They were K8247-K8258 and K8270-K8272. On the 24th Fury K8251 bounced on landing at Mildenhall and overturned. It was repaired and returned to service but otherwise, the Squadron didn't loose any Fury during its serving time with it. It was S/L Eric S Finch posted in from No.7 FTS who became the CO of the Squadron. During the Empire Air Day celebrations 'A' Flight put on displays at Henlow, Halton and Hatfield, while 'B' Flight put on displays at Upper Heyford and Abingdon.

The Squadron had one rather unsavoury character, P/O Neville Heath. He was described as rather moody and disliked by most of the Squadron. At one point he went AWOL for two months. He was later kicked out of the RAF in September 1937. In 1946 he was arrested for the horrific murders of two women, and later hanged at Pentonville Prison in October of that year. In June the Squadron moved to Debden and finally received their Gladiators. The Furies were passed on to various other squadrons.

No.87 Squadron
March 1937 - June 1937

At the same time No.73 Squadron was formed, elements of No.54 Squadron was used to form No.87 Squadron, which was based at Tangmere. They received six Fury Is and thirteen Fury IIs, K7276-K7278, K7281 and K8273-K8281. Five other Fury IIs were also used. These were K8256-K8258 and K8270 and K8271. One Fury II was lost when during a landing at Sutton Bridge when K8277 hit a hedge and overturned, the pilot, F/L Donald E. Turner escaping injuries. Turner later served with No.238 Squadron during the Battle of Britain before being reported missing on 8 August 1940. As for the Fury, it was later written off as being beyond economic repair. As for No.73 Squadron, the association with the Fury was short lived as in June the Squadron moved to Debden and began to re-equip with Gladiators, the last Furies leaving in August.

No.41 Squadron
October 1937 - January 1939

A Demon unit since 1934, No.41 Squadron has been sent to Aden for policing operations in the area and because of the Abysinian Crisis. When it returned to the UK in August 1936 it was based at Catterick. In October 1937 it traded in its Demons for Fury IIs. A total of nineteen Fury IIs were issued to the Squadron. They were K7263-K7266 and K7268-K7278 and K7281-K7283 and K7285. As with the other Fury squadrons display flying became the norm and the Squadron took part in numerous flying displays up and down the country.

During its service with the Squadron, two Mk.IIs were lost in accident. The first occurred on 20 April 1938 when the engine of K7273 cut in flight. The aircraft hit a fence in trying to make a forced landing and overturned at Alwinton, Northumberland during an exercise with Air Observer Corps. Its pilot, P/O Philip D.J. Strong was lucky enough to escape major injuires in the process. The second and last one occurred a couple of weeks before the Fury left the Squadron on 3 November. Returning from an affiliation exercise flight, K7280 flown P/O Horace E.H. Overhall stalled on landing and crashed. Even if the damages were considered as being superficial, K7280 was finally withdrawn from use due to the approaching date of retirement of the type and it became an instructional airframe in March 1939. Overall, a Canadian from Niagara Falls, Ontario, continued to serve with No.41 Squadron and found his death one year later on 6 November 1939 in a flying accident.

late 1938 the Furies started to be replaced by Spitfires and the last Furies left in January 1939. The Furies were passed on to Maintenance Units, although a small number went to No.87 Squadron as replacements.

No.1 Squadron
December 1937 - October 1938

In December 1937, No.1 Squadron was flying Fury Mk.Is since February 1932. It began to take charge of Fury Mk.IIs, as most of the older mark were reaching their airframe time limit. That month, the following Mk.IIs arrived at the Squadron, K8247-K8249, K8255, K8272, K8275-8277, K8279, K8281, K8289, K8291, K8296 and K8303. If some have been previously used by either No.73 or No.87 Squadrons, some came directly from storage. The Mk.II assignment was completed by a handful of Mk.Is and the Squadron continued to fly on Furies until October 1938 when the Squadron was converted onto the Hurricane. The Squadron did not record any major accident during that time.

No.43 Squadron
December 1937 - February 1939

Even it is not known with certitude when the first Fury Mk.II arrived at the Squadron, it is believed that it was more or less at the moment No.1 Squadron took charge of its own Mk.IIs. The Fury Mk.IIs known to have been used by No.43 Squadron are K7275, K8250-8255, K8256, K8257 and K8299. Most have previously served with No.73 or No.87 Squadrons as for No.1. They flew alongside a couple of Mk.Is still in Squadrons'hands, but the year to come was uneventful.

During the Munich Crisis later in 1938 No.43 Squadron was declared a day and night fighter squadron. The Fury was not

K7266 of No.41 Squadron leading K7272 and 7274. Note the absence of any top wing markings, only the squadron insigniabeing painted on the tail.

Hawker Fury K7284 never served with any operational squadron, and was issued one month after its delivery to the RAf in December 1936 to the Station Flight Northolt. Still serving with this Station Flight, it was victim of an engine failure in flight on 28.09.39 and hit trees while making a forced landing. It was struck off charge two weeks later.

equipped for night flying, and except a special flame collector, the Furies did not have any navigation light, cockpit lights or landing flares. However the pilots and ground crew lashed torches to the top port longerons. Downward signalling lamps were found and duly fitted. When Chamberlain declared 'Peace in our time' these lash ups were removed. Which is probably just as well. During November 1938 No.43 Squadron started to receive Hurricanes and their Furies were soon passed on to second line units. The last six Furies were transferred to Kemble in February 1939, missing the outbreak of war of six months.

Miscellaneous units

Contrary to the Mk.I, the Fury MkII didn't have to wait the end of the first-line service to find another usage with the second-line units. Indeed, and from the beginning, the Furies built by General Aircraft found their way into a number of Flying Training Schools to be used for advanced pilot training alongside Fury Mk.Is. By order of allocations, the first to received some Mk.IIs was No.9 FTS (Hullavington), followed by No.6 FTS (Netheravon), No.8 FTS (Montrose), No.10 FTS (Ternhill). Later on some more Flying Training Schools had Fury Mk.IIs in charge and many served as advanced trainer until being retired in 1940. Many fighter pilots who participated to the Battle of France and Battle of Britain flew the Fury during their training syllabus, like Adrian Bouwens, Colin P.N. Brett, James Gillies, Edwin C. Lenton, Stephen Levenson (who later resigned his commission) Ernest Monk, Bernard J. Rofe, Thomas Smart, Donald S. Smithor and some with more

known names like Charles B.F. Kingcome (see list of accident). Some others Furies also saw service with the Central Flying School at Upavon, or Royal Air Force College or served at various Station Flights. When the war broke out, about 60 Mk.IIs were still in service mainly as trainers at various places. However, the majority of them were already approaching their time-limit airframe and with the need to respond to the new air war which had already given many lessons, more modern aircraft were called to fulfil the advanced training role, and consequently the Furies were withdrawn from use in 1940. Many were converted to ground instructional airframe, making and end to the career of the probably most elegant British fighter of the inter-war period.

The fate of many Fury Mk.IIs at the end of their service life, becoming an instructional airframe. Here a former No.43 Sqn machine.

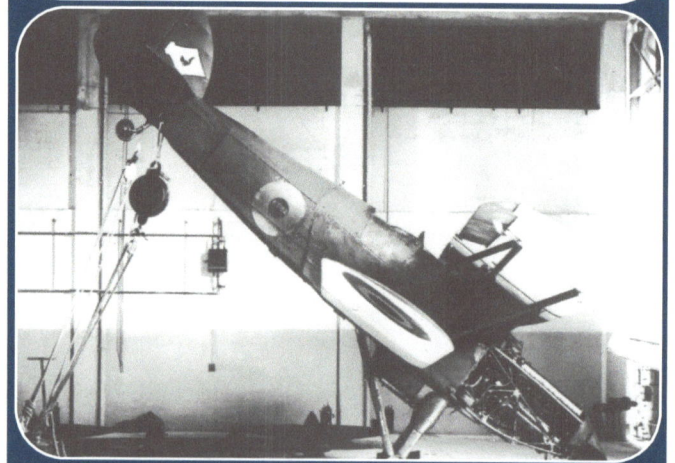

This page and next: No.43 Squadron flying over the cloud with a new camouflage painted on the aircraft recently introduced for the Munich crises in 1938. Only remains the Squadron's insignia on the tail, however, not all aircraft.

Date	Unit	Pilot	SN	Origin	Serial	Fate
02.01.37	No.9 FTS	P/O Bonar R. WHALEY	RAF No.?	RAF	K8221	-
22.01.37	Cranwell ATS	S/L Francis R.D. SWAIN	RAF No.17018	RAF	K8260	-
21.04.37	No.6 FTS	LAC Leonard HOPKIRK	RAF No.565173	RAF	K8234	-
26.04.37	No.25 Sqn	Sgt Ernest W.J. MONK	RAF No.564342	RAF	K7267	-
14.05.37	No.9 FTS	P/O Stephen A. LEVENSON	RAF No.?	RAF	K8220	-
21.05.37	No.87 Sqn	F/L Douglas E. TURNER	RAF No.32254	RAF	K8277	-
29.05.37	No.2 FTS	S/L Henry E. POWER	RAF No.?	RAF	K8228	†
12.06.37	No.9 FTS	F/O Alfred A. McMATH	RAF No.?	RAF	K8219	†
03.08.37	No.25 Sqn	P/O Lloyd K. KEITH	RAF No.?	RAF	K7279	-
19.11.37	No.7 FTS	P/O Colin P.N. BRETT	RAF No.39850	RAF	K8270	-
01.12.37	No.6 FTS	LAC Rene A. ALBONICO	RAF No.515773	RAF	K8258	-
18.01.38	No.8 FTS	P/O James H.L. ALLEN	RAF No.39957	RAF	K8263	-
14.02.38	No.10 FTS	P/O Richard A. RANSLEY	RAF No.47544	RAF	K8286	-
09.03.38	CFS	2/Lt Mohammed M. ISMAIL		EAAF*	K8241	-
20.04.38	No.41 Sqn	P/O Philip D.J. STRONG	RAF No.37699	RAF	K7273	-
25.05.38	No.9 FTS	P/O Andrew K. HUNTER	RAF No.36113	RAF	K8223	-
27.06.38	RAFC	Flt Cdt Charles B.F. KINGCOMBE	RAF No.33319	RAF	K8302	-
28.06.38	No.10 FTS	P/O Thomas SMART	RAF No.40324	RAF	K8282	-
21.10.38	No.11 FTS	P/O John L. COLD WELLS	RAF No.40675	RAF	K8235	-
27.10.38	No.2 AAC	P/O Arthur M.L. ALDERTON	RAF No.40066	RAF	K8280	-
31.10.38	No.7 FTS	P/O Donald S. SMITH	RAF No.40859	RAF	K8251	-
03.11.38	No.41 Sqn	P/O Horace E.H. OVERALL	RAF No.39331	(CAN)/RAF	K7288	-
10.12.38	No.9 FTS	Cpl John R. DANIEL	RAF No.566250	RAF	K8275	†
20.03.39	No.11 FTS	LAC James GILLIES	RAF No.519573	RAF	K8294	-
	No.7 FTS	P/O Edwin C. LENTON	RAF No.41187	RAF	K8224	-
29.03.39	No.8 FTS	F/O Douglas E.A. WILLIAMS	RAF No.37581	RAF	K8253	-
04.05.39	RAFC	Flt Cdt Adrian BOUWENS	RAF No.33420	RAF	K8301	-
20.06.39	No.9 FTS	P/O Eric R. McGOVERN	RAF No.?	RAF	K8222	†
28.09.39	SF Northolt	P/O Michael H. ANDERSON (1)	AAF No.90497	RAF	K7284	-
13.11.39	No.1 AAS	F/L Ernest H. JAGO	RAF No.36076	RAF	K8244	†
18.02.40	No.8 FTS	1st Off S.E. CUMMINGS	ATA	RAF	K8304	-
23.02.40	No.2 FTS	F/L John St.C. ARBUTHNOTT	RAF No.22059	RAF	K8227	-
17.03.40	SF Notholt	F/O George V. PROUDMAN (2)	RAF No.39947	RAF	K8257	-

(1) pilot from No.600 Sqn

(2) pilot from No.65 Sqn

* Egyptian Army Air Force

Total: 33

GROUND INSTRUCTIONAL AIRFRAME

K7266	12.05.38	Believed time-expired. To 1065M
K8235	13.12.38	To 1195M following accident.
K8247	07.06.39	Believed time-expired. To 1546M
K8248	07.06.39	Believed time-expired. To 1553M
K8249	07.06.39	Believed time-expired. To 1547M
K8272	07.06.39	Believed time-expired. To 1552M
K8276	07.06.39	Believed time-expired. To 1548M
K8279	07.06.39	Believed time-expired. To 1551M
K8281	07.06.39	Believed time-expired. To 1549M
K8296	07.06.39	Believed time-expired. To 1550M
K7263	08.06.39	Believed time-expired. To 1569M
K7264	08.06.39	Believed time-expired. To 1570M
K7266	08.06.39	Believed time-expired. To 1571M
K7268	08.06.39	Believed time-expired. To 1572M
K7269	08.06.39	Believed time-expired. To 1573M
K7270	08.06.39	Believed time-expired. To 1574M

K7271	08.06.39	Believed time-expired. To 1575M
K7277	08.06.39	Believed time-expired. To 1576M
K7281	08.06.39	Believed time-expired. To 1577M, later 2318M 05.11.40
K7282	08.06.39	Believed time-expired. To 1578M
K7285	08.06.39	Believed time-expired. To 1579M
K8273	06.09.39	Believed time-expired. To 1644M
K8280	06.09.39	Believed time-expired. To 1643M
K8225	17.01.40	Believed time-expired. To 1731M
K8226	17.01.40	Believed time-expired. To 1715M
K8227	?	To 1725M following accident.
K8230	17.01.40	Believed time-expired. To 1716M
K8231	17.01.40	Believed time-expired. To 1729M
K8232	17.01.40	Believed time-expired. To 1726M
K8233	17.01.40	Believed time-expired. To 1717M
K8237	17.01.40	Believed time-expired. To 1733M
K8242	17.01.40	Believed time-expired. To 1740M
K8250	17.01.40	Believed time-expired. To 1734M
K8252	17.01.40	Believed time-expired. To 1712M
K8255	17.01.40	Believed time-expired. To 1737M
K8259	17.01.40	Believed time-expired. To 1741M
K8261	17.01.40	Believed time-expired. To 1740M
K8262	17.01.40	Believed time-expired. To 1740M
k8265	17.01.40	Believed time-expired. To 1707M
K8266	17.01.40	Believed time-expired. To 1708M
K8267	17.01.40	Believed time-expired. To 1709M
K8268	17.01.40	Believed time-expired. To 1724M
K8269	17.01.40	Believed time-expired. To 1727M
K8275	17.01.40	Believed time-expired. To 1711M
K8278	17.01.40	Believed time-expired. To 1714M
K8283	17.01.40	Believed time-expired. To 1720M
K8284	17.01.40	Believed time-expired. To 1721M
K8286	17.01.40	Believed time-expired. To 1722M
K8287	17.01.40	Believed time-expired. To 1724M
K8288	17.01.40	Believed time-expired. To 1718M
K8293	17.01.40	Believed time-expired. To 1704M
K8295	17.01.40	Believed time-expired. To 1735M
K8297	17.01.40	Believed time-expired. To 1728M
K8298	17.01.40	Believed time-expired. To 1723M
K8299	17.01.40	Believed time-expired. To 1713M
K8306	17.01.40	Believed time-expired. To 1736M
K8304	?	To 1706M following accident.
K8256	28.02.40	Believed time-expired. To 1823M
K8290	28.02.40	Believed time-expired. To 1824M
K8291	13.03.40	Believed time-expired. To 1847M
K8218	27.04.40	Believed time-expired. To 1912M
K8240	27.04.40	Believed time-expired. To 1910M
K8254	27.04.40	Believed time-expired. To 1913M
K8264	27.04.40	Believed time-expired. To 1914M
K8285	27.04.40	Believed time-expired. To 1915M
K8303	27.04.40	Believed time-expired. To 1916M
K8305	27.04.40	Believed time-expired. To 1909M
K8238	10.05.40	Believed time-expired. To 1918M
K8239	10.05.40	Believed time-expired. To 1920M
K8292	10.05.40	Believed time-expired. To 1919M
K7265	18.06.40	Believed time-expired. To 2033M
K7272	18.06.40	Believed time-expired. To 2027M
K7274	18.06.40	Believed time-expired. To 2031M
K7275	18.06.40	Believed time-expired. To 2032M
K7283	20.09.40	Believed time-expired. To 2230M, later 2240M 10.10.40
K8246	31.07.40	Believed time-expired. To 1948M

Fury K8280 was serving with No.2 AACU when during a flight, the engine cut and K8280 tipped up on landing on the beach at Hayling Island (Hants). It returned on service after repairs and eventually became an instructional airframe.

Serials		Date on Sqn	Date off Sqn
K7263:	25 Sqn	02.10.36	*Oct-37*
	41 Sqn	*Oct-37*	*Jan-39*
K7264:	25 Sqn	02.10.36	*Oct-37*
	41 Sqn	*Oct-37*	04.11.37
K7265:	25 Sqn	02.10.36	*Oct-37*
	41 Sqn	*Oct-37*	*Jan-39*

Fury K7265 of No.41 Sqn at an unknown date, but probably early in its service with this unkit at the end of 1937. Note the blue tail with the squadron insignia and the total absence of wing markings nor the usual fuselage red band reserved for No.41 Sqn. *(Chris Goss)*

Serials		Date on Sqn	Date off Sqn
K7266:	25 Sqn	02.10.36	*Oct-37*
	41 Sqn	?	*Jan-39*
K7267:	25 Sqn	02.10.36	*Oct-37*
K7268:	25 Sqn	02.10.37	*Oct-37*
	41 Sqn	*Oct-37*	*Jan-39*
K7269:	25 Sqn	02.10.36	*Oct-37*
	41 Sqn	*Oct-37*	*Jan-39*
K7270:	25 Sqn	02.10.36	*Oct-37*
	41 Sqn	*Oct-37*	*Jan-39*
K7271:	25 Sqn	02.10.36	*Oct-37*
	41 Sqn	*Oct-37*	*Jan-39*
K7272:	25 Sqn	02.10.36	*Oct-37*
	41 Sqn	*Oct-37*	*Jan-39*
K7273:	25 Sqn	02.10.36	*Oct-37*
	41 Sqn	*Oct-37*	20.04.38
K7274:	25 Sqn	02.10.36	*Oct-37*
	41 Sqn	*Oct-37*	*Jan-39*
K7275:	25 Sqn	02.10.36	*Oct-37*
	41 Sqn	*Oct-37*	?
	43 Sqn	?	06.02.39
K7276:	25 Sqn	02.10.36	?
	41 Sqn	*Oct-37*	?
	87 Sqn	15.03.37	*Jun-37*
K7277:	41 Sqn	?	?
	87 Sqn	15.03.37	*Jun-37*

Fury K7270 while in service with No.25 Sqn. The tail is painted in red and was the aircraft of the A Flight leader. *(Phil Jarrett)*

Fury K7275 of No. 25 Sqn with its full squadron markings. This squadron is probably the only one with No.1 Sqn to have worn its markings in full on its Fury Mk.IIs.

Fury K7279 of No.25 Sqn seen while ready for take-off with K7264. K7279 was later lost in an accident.

Fury K7280 of No.25 Sqn in flight in 1937. If the Fury was still an elegant aircraft, it was outclassed by more modern fighter which were put into service in the World in the same time the Mk.II was put into service.

Fury K7281 served a short time with No.41 Sqn

Fury K7284 of the Station Flight Northolt in 1937 - 1938. Note the total lack of markings. When it was wrecked in an accident in September 1939, it was still serving at SF Northolt. However, nothing is known about its camouflage and markings at that time.
(Andrew Thomas)

K7278:	41 Sqn	?	?
	87 Sqn	15.03.37	*Jun-37*
K7279:	25 Sqn	03.11.36	03.08.37
K7280:	25 Sqn	03.11.36	?
	41 Sqn	?	03.11.38
K7281:	25 Sqn	03.11.36	?
	41 Sqn	?	?
	87 Sqn	15.03.37	*Jun-37*
K7282:	25 Sqn	?	?
	41 Sqn	?	28.02.38
K7283:	25 Sqn	?	?
	41 Sqn	?	*Jan-39*
K7284:	-		
K7285:	41 Sqn	?	*Jan-39*
K8218:	-		
K8219:	-		
K8220:	-		
K8221:	-		
K8222:	-		

Fury K8222 seen while serving with No.9 FTS in Spring 1939. This Fury only served this Flying Training School from July 1936 onwards before being in lost in a flying accident in June 1939 killing its pilot - see colour profile.
(*Andrew Thomas*)

K8223:	-
K8224:	-
K8225:	-
K8226:	-
K8227:	-
K8228:	-
K8229:	-
K8230:	-
K8231:	-
K8232:	-
K8233:	-
K8234:	-
K8235:	-
K8236:	-
K8237:	-
K8238:	-
K8239:	-
K8240:	-

While landing at Penrhos, the undercarriage collapsed and putting an end to the career of K8234. The pilot escaped injuries. This Fury was serving at No.6 FTS when the accident occurred
- see colour profile -

It is not known exactly when K8249 was issued to No.1 Sqn, but surely when No.73 Sqn relinquished its Furies for Gladiators in June 1937. It is flying with its full squadron markings in usage in 1937.

K8241:	-		
K8242:	-		
K8243:	-		
K8244:	-		
K8245:	-		
K8246:	-		
K8247:	73 Sqn	15.03.37	*Jun-37*
	1 Sqn	?	*Oct-38*
K8248:	73 Sqn	15.03.37	*Jun-37*
	1 Sqn	?	*Oct-38*
K8249:	73 Sqn	15.03.37	*Jun-37*
	1 Sqn	?	*Oct-38*
K8250:	73 Sqn	15.03.37	*Jun-37*
	43 Sqn	?	?
K8251:	73 Sqn	15.03.37	*Jun-37*
	43 Sqn	?	?
K8252:	73 Sqn	15.03.37	*Jun-37*
	43 Sqn	?	06.02.39
K8253:	73 Sqn	15.03.37	*Jun-37*
	43 Sqn	?	06.02.39
K8254:	73 Sqn	15.03.37	*Jun-37*

Hawker Fury K8238 was delivered to the Central Flying School directly from the manufacturer in November 1936. This Fury ended its carer as an instructional airframe in May 1940. *(Phil Jarrett)*

	43 Sqn	?	*Jan-39*
K8255:	73 Sqn	15.03.37	*Jun-37*
	1 Sqn	?	*Oct-38*
K8256:	73 Sqn	15.03.37	*Jun-37*
	87 Sqn	?	?
	43 Sqn	?	?
K8257:	73 Sqn	15.03.37	*Jun-37*
	87 Sqn	?	?
	43 Sqn	?	?
K8258:	73 Sqn	15.03.37	*Jun-37*
	87 Sqn	?	?
K8259:	-		
K8260:	-		
K8261:	-		
K8262:	-		
K8263:	-		
K8264:	-		
K8265:	-		
K8266:	-		
K8267:	-		

Formation practice for three pilots of No.8 FTS over the snowy British countryside. All three were damaged in various accident but all were able to return to service.
- see colour profile -

K8268:	-	03.11.32	04.01.34
K8269:	-	29.11.33	21.12.36
K8270:	73 Sqn	15.03.37	*Jun-37*
	87 Sqn	?	?
K8271:	73 Sqn	15.03.37	*Jun-37*
	87 Sqn	?	?
K8272:	73 Sqn	15.03.37	*Jun-37*
	1 Sqn	?	*Oct-38*
K8273:	87 Sqn	15.03.37	*Jun-37*
K8274:	87 Sqn	15.03.37	*Jun-37*
K8275:	87 Sqn	15.03.37	12.08.37
	1 Sqn	10.12.37	27.10.38
K8276:	87 Sqn	15.03.37	*Jun-37*
	1 Sqn	10.12.37	*Oct-38*
K8277:	87 Sqn	15.03.37	21.05.37
K8278:	87 Sqn	15.03.37	*Jun-37*
	1 Sqn	10.12.37	?

K8279:	87 Sqn	15.03.37	12.08.37
	1 Sqn	10.12.37	*Oct-38*
K8280:	87 Sqn	15.03.37	12.08.37
	1 Sqn	10.12.37	?
K8281:	87 Sqn	15.03.37	12.08.37
	1 Sqn	10.12.37	*Oct-38*
K8282:	-		
K8283:	-		
K8284:	-		
K8285:	-		
K8286:	-		
K8287:	-		
K8288:	-		
K8289:	1 Sqn	?	*Oct-38*
K8290:	1 Sqn	?	*Oct-38*
K8291:	1 Sqn	?	*Oct-38*
K8292:	-		
K8293:	-		
K8294:	-		
K8295:	-		
K8296:	1 Sqn	?	*Oct-38*
K8297:	-		
K8298:	-		
K8299:	43 Sqn	?	*Nov-38*
K8300:	-		
K8301:	-		
K8302:	-		
K8303:	1 Sqn	?	*Oct-38*
K8304:	-		
K8305:	-		
K8306:	-		

Fury K8276 served only a shirt time with No.1 Sqn. It is seen before the Munich Crisis still wearing the red fuselage bands. Note the squadron insignia on the fin.

Fury Mk.IIs of No.25 Squadron in flight, the CO leading.

†

ROLL OF HONOUR
FURY MK.II

Name	Rank	Age	Origin	Date	Serial
DANIEL, John Robert	Cpl	22	RAF	10.12.38	K8275
JAGO, Ernest Henry	F/L	38	RAF	13.11.39	K8244
McGOVERN, Eric R.	P/O	21	RAF	20.06.39	K8244
McMATH, Alfred Archibald	F/O	*n/k*	RAF	12.06.37	K8219
POWER, Harry Eustace	S/L	*n/k*	RAF	29.05.37	K8228

Total:

RAF: 5

n/k : not known

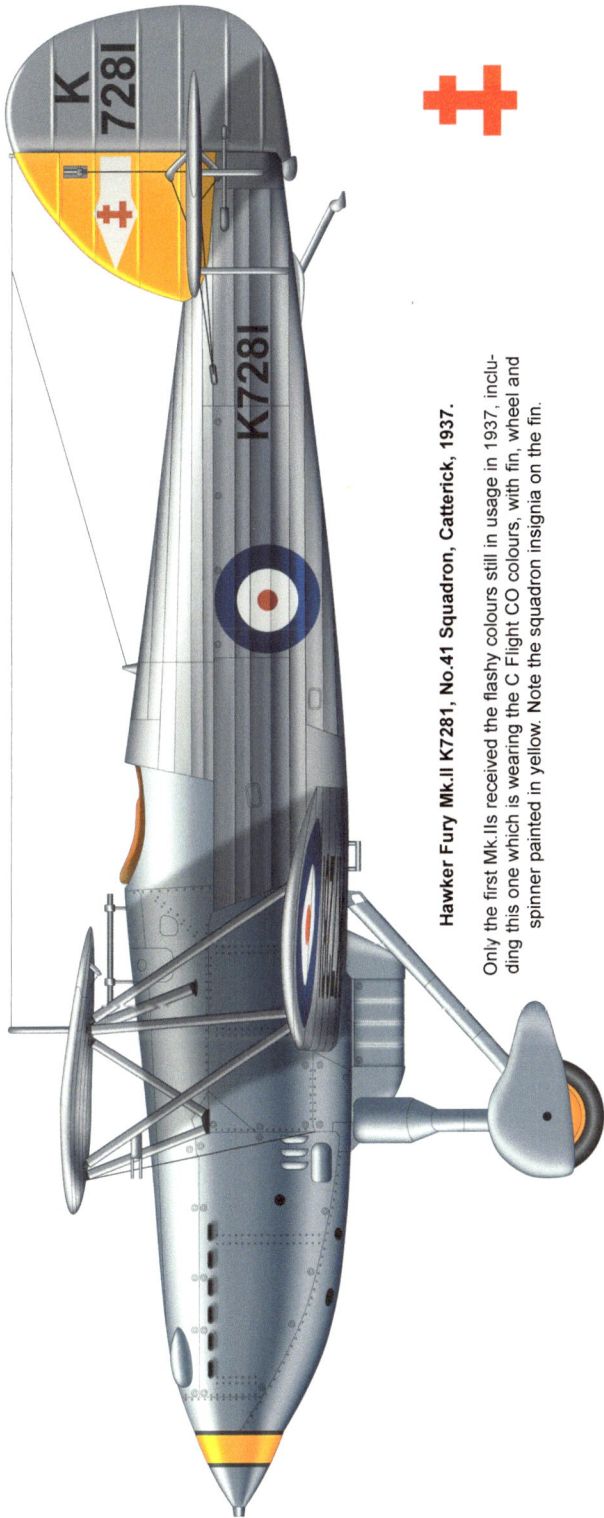

Hawker Fury Mk.II K7281, No.41 Squadron, Catterick, 1937.

Only the first Mk.IIs received the flashy colours still in usage in 1937, including this one which is wearing the C Flight CO colours, with fin, wheel and spinner painted in yellow. Note the squadron insignia on the fin.

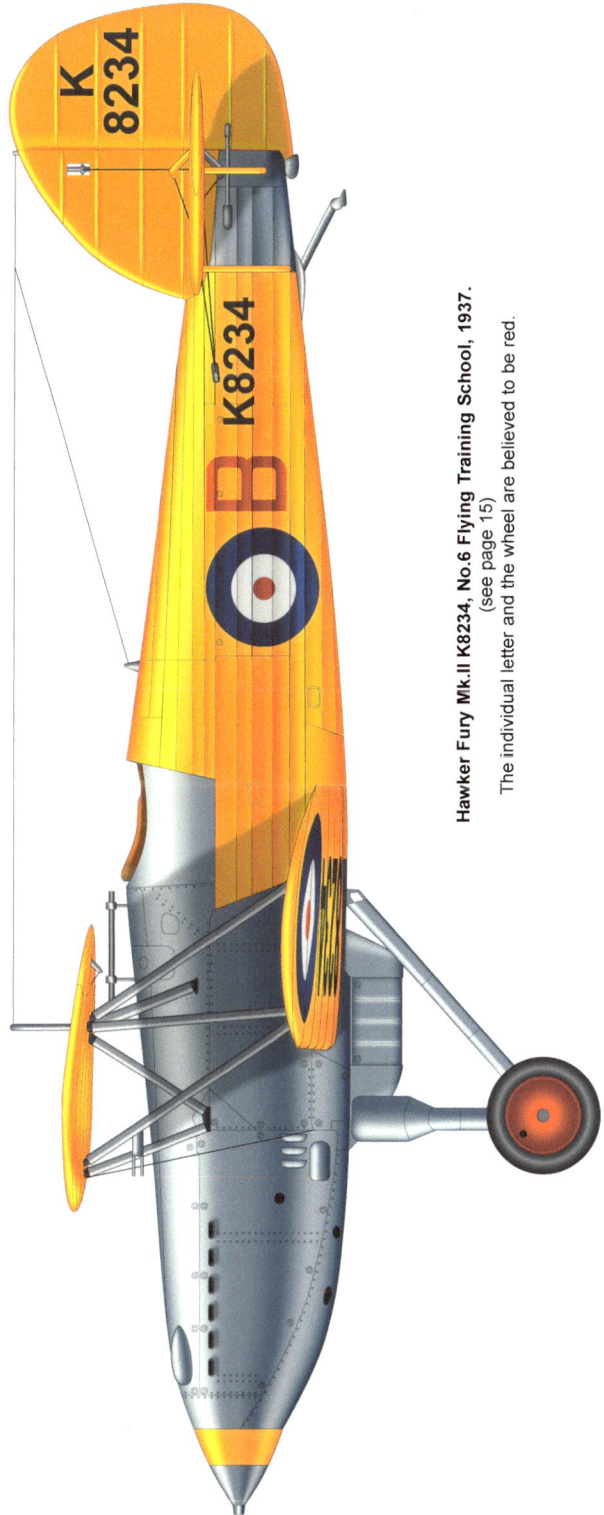

Hawker Fury Mk.II K8234, No.6 Flying Training School, 1937.
(see page 15)
The individual letter and the wheel are believed to be red.

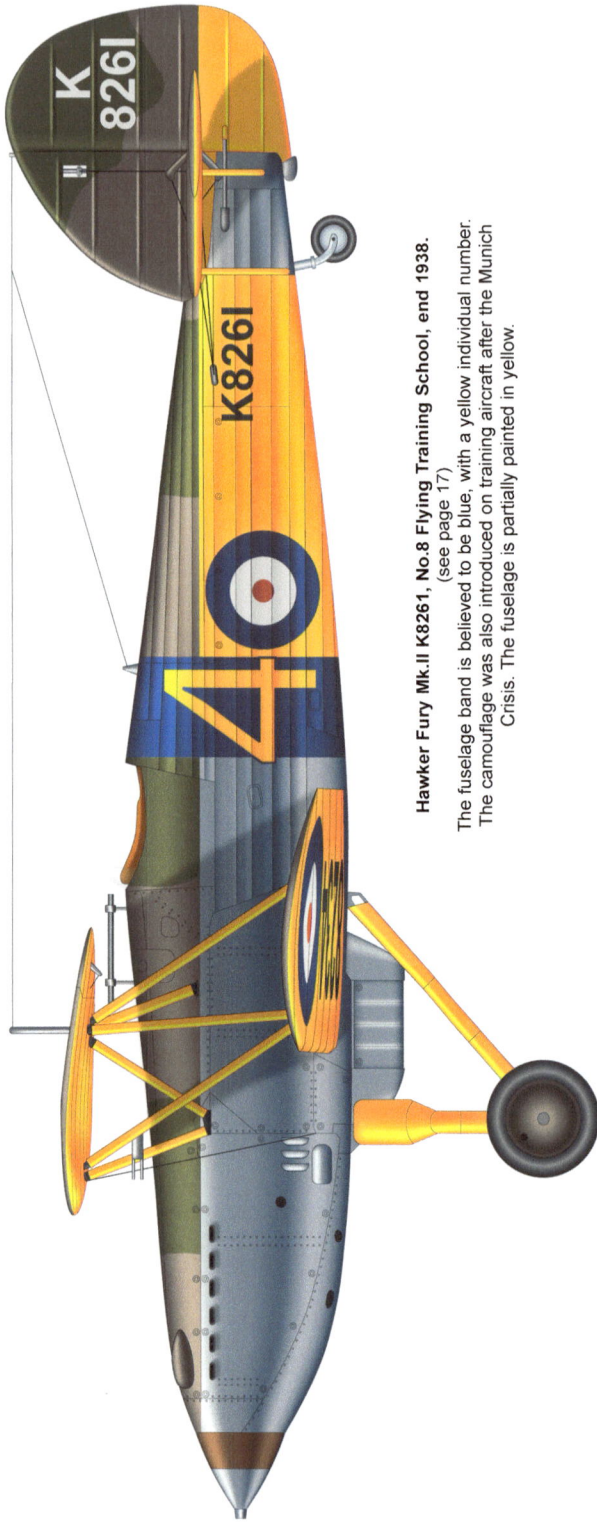

Hawker Fury Mk.II K8261, No.8 Flying Training School, end 1938.
(see page 17)
The fuselage band is believed to be blue, with a yellow individual number. The camouflage was also introduced on training aircraft after the Munich Crisis. The fuselage is partially painted in yellow.

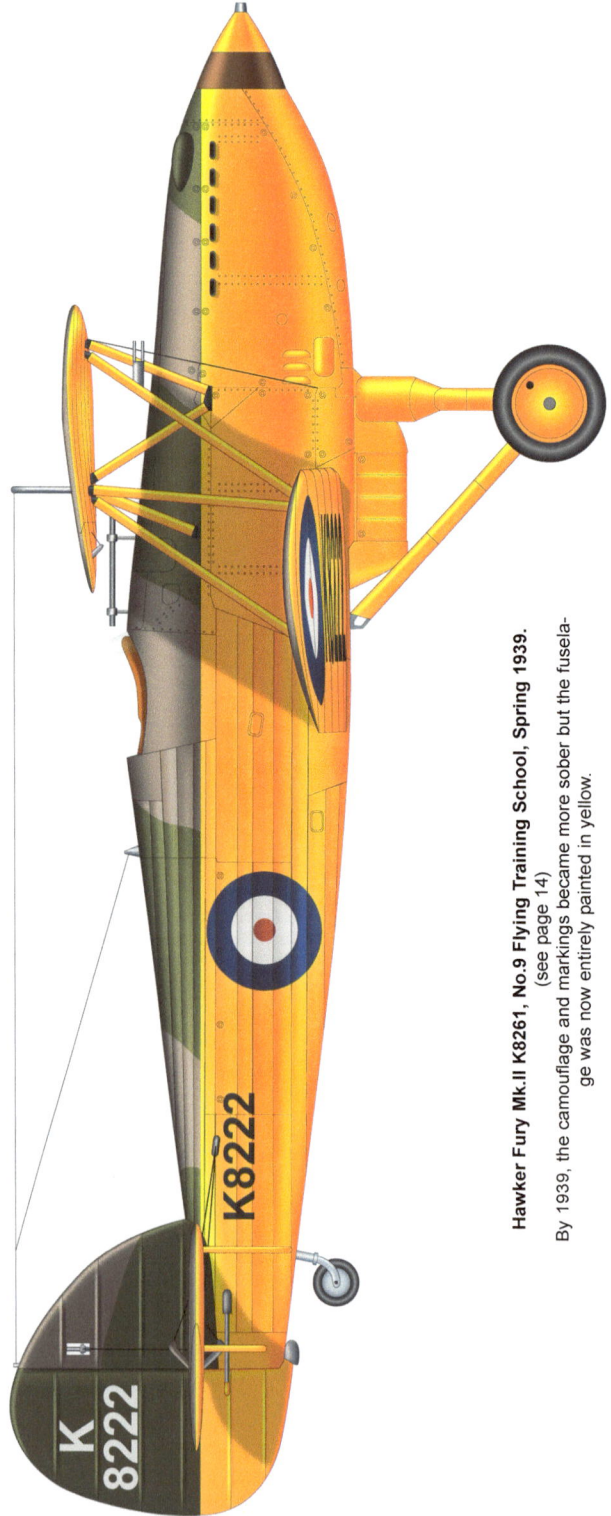

Hawker Fury Mk.II K8261, No.9 Flying Training School, Spring 1939.
(see page 14)
By 1939, the camouflage and markings became more sober but the fuselage was now entirely painted in yellow.

Hawker Fury Mk.II serial unknown, No.43 Squadron, Tangmere, 1938.
(see page 7 & 8)

During the Munich Crisis, all the fighters were given a camouflage scheme of dark earth/dark dark green upper surfaces, while the undersurfaces of the wings were white/night and the fuselage and tailplane aluminium.

Only the Squadron badge - but not on all Furies - , a Gamecock, was retained on the fin within a white spearhead.

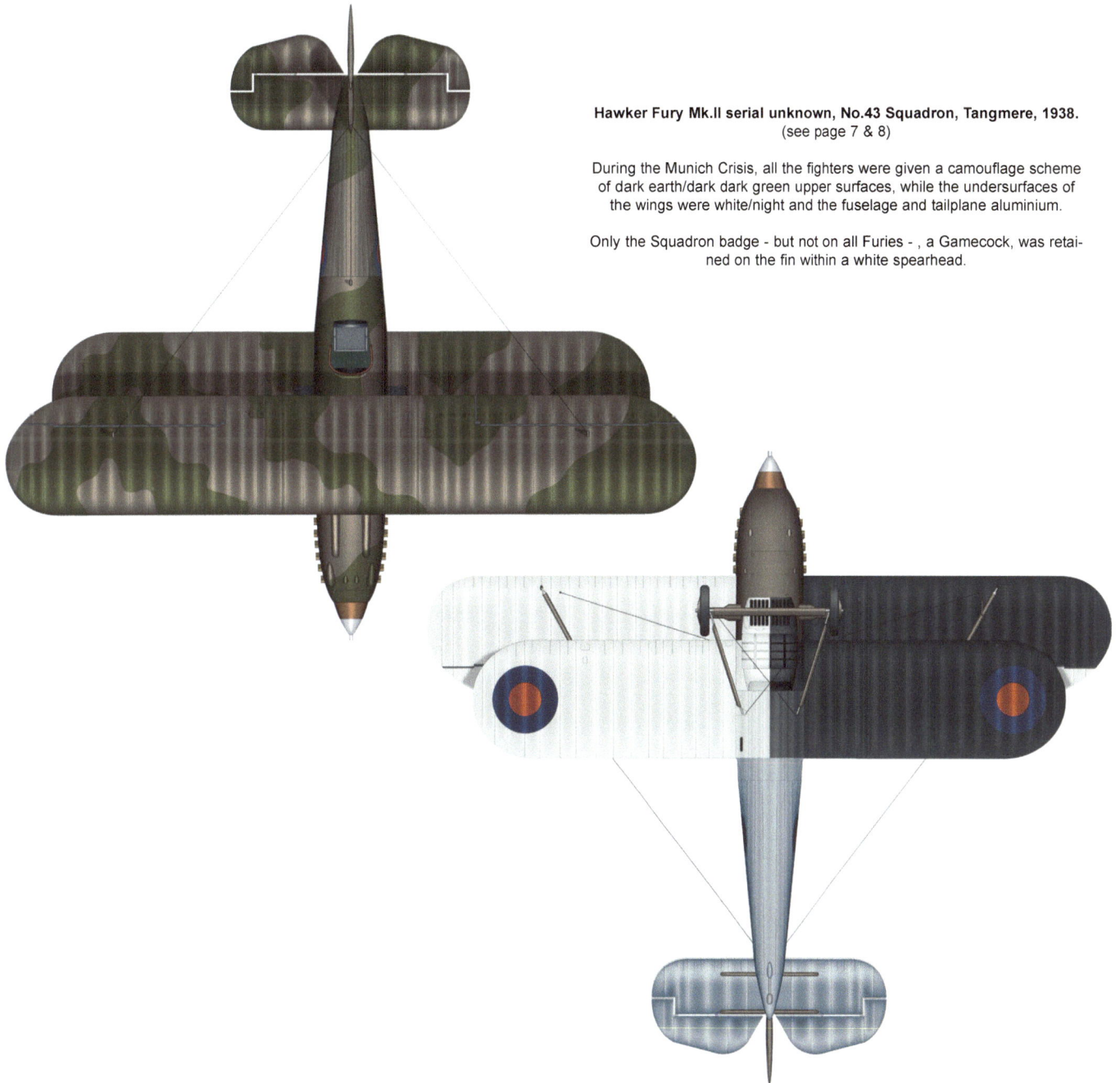

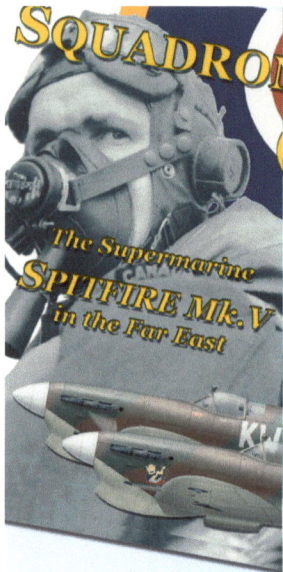

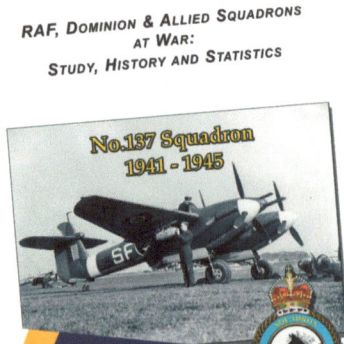

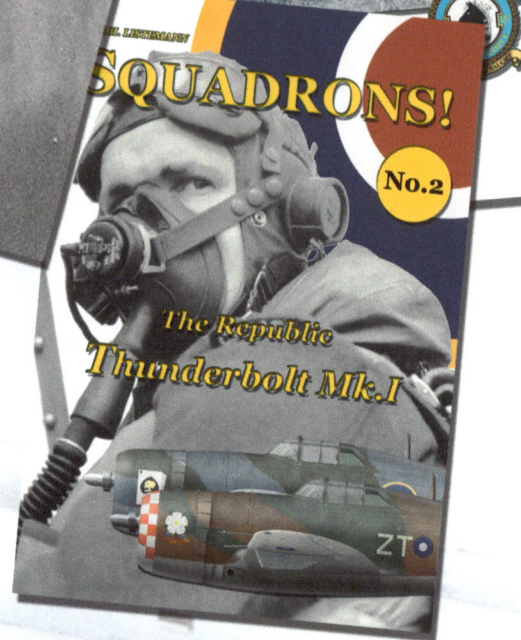

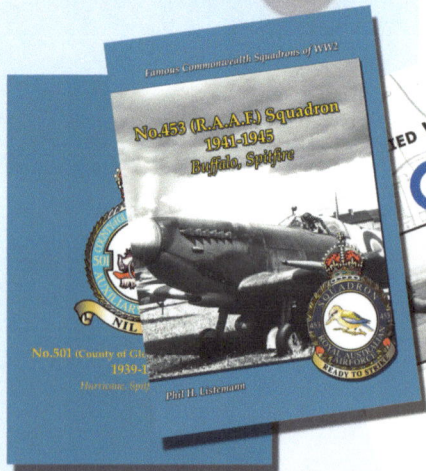

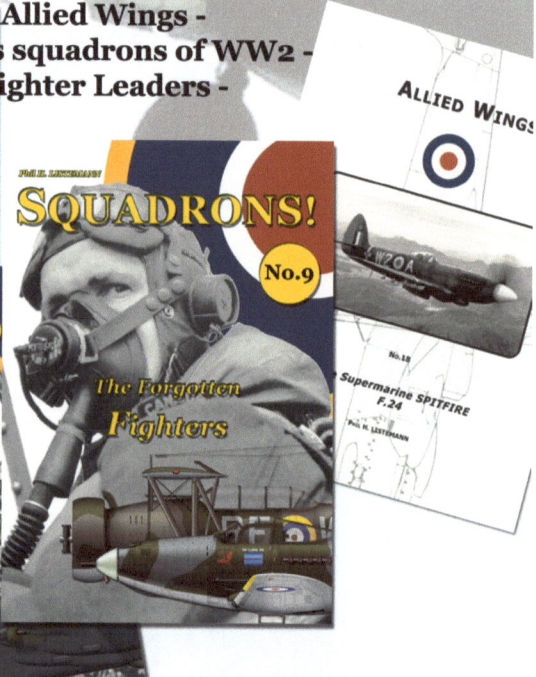

www.ingramcontent.com/pod-product-compliance
Lightning Source LLC
LaVergne TN
LVHW072117070426
835510LV00002B/94